Original title:
The Great Sleepy Adventure

Copyright © 2024 Creative Arts Management OÜ
All rights reserved.

Author: Christian Leclair
ISBN HARDBACK: 978-9916-90-360-5
ISBN PAPERBACK: 978-9916-90-361-2

A Sleepwalker's Delightful Detour

Under moonlight's gentle glow,
Steps wander where the shadows flow.
Fields of whispers, secrets breathe,
In the night, the heart takes leave.

Paths entwined in silver light,
Dance with stars, spirits in flight.
Each turn a story, lost in time,
Melodies of dreams, sweet as rhyme.

Lost in the Labyrinth of Dreams

In the maze where visions play,
Twisting thoughts drift far away.
Echoes call from corridors,
As sleep unveils its hidden doors.

Faces blend, and shapes distort,
In a realm where shadows court.
Each thread woven, calm yet bold,
A tapestry of dreams unfolds.

The Sleepy Sky's Hidden Paths

Up above, the starlight weaves,
Gentle glows that hush the leaves.
Clouds like cushions, soft they lie,
Cradling wishes drifting by.

Moonlit trails and comet's glide,
Where tired wishes sway and hide.
In the quiet, hearts will soar,
Seeking peace forevermore.

Echoes of Dreams Amidst the Stars

Whispers float on twilight's breeze,
Carried softly through the trees.
Every twinkle holds a tale,
Of moonlit journeys, soft and pale.

From the depths of slumber's sea,
Come the echoes, wild and free.
In the night, the stars align,
To guide the dreamer, as they shine.

Gentle Ripples on Sleep's Surface

In twilight's calm, the whispers flow,
Soft blankets wrap the world below.
Dreams drift like leaves upon the stream,
A tranquil heart, a fleeting dream.

Stars blink above in silent grace,
Time slows down, a slow embrace.
With every sigh, the night unfolds,
The magic of the dark it holds.

Moonlight spills on slumber's face,
Guiding souls to a peaceful place.
Each breath a wave, gentle and light,
On sleep's surface, all feels right.

The Enigma of Cozy Nights

The evening sighs, a hearth aglow,
Whispers of warmth in the gentle flow.
Beneath the covers, secrets reside,
In cozy corners, dreams abide.

Shadows dance on walls so wide,
While thoughts and wishes take a ride.
Sipping stories, the world slows down,
In the soft embrace of twilight's gown.

Candlelight flickers, time drifts by,
As comfort wraps like a lullaby.
In the embrace of a night so deep,
We find the treasures that memories keep.

Adventures in a Pillow Fortress

A fortress built with fluff and care,
Soft clouds rising, a secret lair.
In battles fought with dreams in tow,
Each pillow holds a tale to sow.

Crisp sheets wave like banners bright,
As imagination takes to flight.
Knights and dragons roam the air,
In this safe space, without a care.

Beneath the stars, the world feels small,
Within the fortress, we stand tall.
Laughter echoes in the night,
In our kingdom, everything's right.

Comet Trails of Drowsiness

The night sky glows with streaks of light,
Whispers of dreams take gentle flight.
Comets blaze through realms unknown,
Guiding weary hearts back home.

Each trail a promise, shimmering bright,
Leading lost souls through the night.
In wonder, we gaze at patterns so grand,
As drowsiness pulls with a soft hand.

Threads of sleep weave tales anew,
In cosmic dance, dreams come true.
With every blink, the world melts away,
In comet trails, we long to stay.

Enchanted Meadow of Heavy Lids

In the meadow where dreams bloom,
Soft whispers cradle the night,
Moonlit petals gently loom,
Stars twinkle in soothing light.

Gentle breezes kiss your brow,
Fluttering shadows play and dance,
In this realm, all is allowed,
Wrapped in a sweet, soft trance.

Dewdrops glisten on soft grass,
Each one a wish waiting to soar,
Time slows down as moments pass,
In silence, we yearn for more.

Restful hearts find peace anew,
As heavy lids begin to close,
In the magic of dreams, we flew,
Awake in a world that glows.

Adventures on Pillows of Cloud

On pillows soft as silken skies,
We glide through realms of pure delight,
With laughter echoing, we rise,
Chasing colors of dreamy light.

Each cloud a castle, fresh and wide,
Where elephants and fairies play,
Guide your heart with childlike pride,
On adventurous paths we sway.

Dancing over stars of silver hue,
With each swoop, we laugh and cheer,
The joy of flying feels so true,
As worries fade into the rear.

In the land where dreams reside,
Together we weave tales so bright,
On pillows of cloud, side by side,
We drift into the velvet night.

The Dream Weaver's Secret Passage

In twilight's cloak, the weaver sings,
Threads of silver, gold, and fate,
With gentle hands, she crafts our wings,
In a passage where dreams await.

Silent echoes of wishes made,
Looming shadows softly sway,
Through the arch of the glade,
To where night meets the day.

A tapestry of stars unfolds,
Whispers of secrets run so deep,
In stories woven, bright and bold,
In this passage, we find our sleep.

Down the corridor of light,
Guided by the moon's soft grace,
We dance through shadows of the night,
In the weaver's warm embrace.

Wanderlust in the Realm of Rest

In dreams, we roam the world so vast,
With restless hearts and open eyes,
Through forests deep and skies so cast,
We journey where the spirit flies.

Mountains call with peaks of wonder,
Oceans shimmer, whispers near,
Each adventure pulls us like thunder,
In the realm where hearts hold dear.

Sparkling trails through starlit nights,
With every step, a wish takes flight,
In this realm, our souls ignite,
Wanderlust guides us with pure light.

As dawn approaches, dreams must fade,
Yet still we carry the magic within,
For every moment, a memory made,
In the realm of rest, we begin.

Beneath the Blanket of Whimsy

Stars twinkle like dreams at night,
Whispers of magic take flight.
Moonlight dances on the streams,
Carrying secrets, hopes, and dreams.

Clouds wear coats of silver lace,
Embracing shadows with a grace.
The world is painted in soft hues,
Where laughter mingles with the blues.

Breezes sing a gentle tune,
Calling forth the brave and bold.
Underneath the yonder moon,
Stories of the heart unfold.

Join the wanderers on this quest,
Where every journey feels like rest.
Hand in hand, we'll boldly tread,
Beneath the blanket of dreams spread.

Restful Roads to Nowhere

Winding paths through emerald fields,
Free your mind, the heart it yields.
Each step whispers tales untold,
In the warmth of earth's soft hold.

Hazy suns and skies of blue,
Guide us to adventures new.
Gentle breezes kiss our skin,
In this realm, we lose to win.

No destination set in stone,
Just the journey, heart alone.
With open hearts and souls so free,
We'll find our place, just you and me.

Calm will cradle our weary feet,
On restful roads, our spirits greet.
With every turn, let's drift along,
In the silence, we belong.

The Land Where Fantasies Dwell

In fields of stars where wishes bloom,
Dreams take flight and banish gloom.
Mountains made of candy bright,
Shimmering under the soft moonlight.

Horizon calls with colors bold,
Tales of magic yet untold.
Rivers flow with laughter sweet,
Guiding us with every beat.

Glimmering fairies dance and play,
Chasing shadows of the day.
In this land where wishes go,
The seeds of joy begin to grow.

Here the heart finds peace and rest,
In every dream, we feel the best.
Where fantasies and hopes align,
A lovely world, forever mine.

Fables from the Land of Nod

Whispers rustle in the night,
Tales of wonder, pure delight.
Dreams are woven, soft and bright,
In the land where shadows light.

Tiny creatures roam the glade,
Sharing secrets, unafraid.
Every star a story spun,
In this realm where dreams are fun.

Clouds become the sailors bold,
Sailing seas of tales retold.
Fables drift on moonlit streams,
Awakening our hidden dreams.

In the land of sleep, we find,
Magic threads that bind the mind.
Close your eyes, let visions flow,
Fables from the land we know.

Dreambound Journeys to Silken Horizons

In dreams we sail on silken seas,
Where whispers of the softest breeze.
Each wave a thought, serene and clear,
We chase horizons, far and near.

With colors bright, our minds will play,
Creating worlds where shadows sway.
In this vast realm of endless night,
We find our dreams take splendid flight.

Where Sleepy Stars Begin to Twinkle

Beneath a sky of velvet blue,
The stars awake, and dreams ensue.
In sleepy towns, the world is still,
With gentle night, our hearts fulfill.

The twinkling lights, they wink and gleam,
As shadows weave a soft, sweet dream.
We drift along the cosmic flow,
Where sleepy stars begin to glow.

Nighttime Quest for the Mysterious Rest

The moonlight shines, a guiding spark,
In quests for rest, we leave our mark.
With every sigh, our burdens fade,
As thoughts of nightlike peace parade.

Through winding paths of silver dreams,
We search for solace, or so it seems.
In realms unknown, we find our way,
In shadows deep where worries sway.

Beneath the Gaze of Lullaby Lights

The night unfolds its tranquil grace,
Beneath the stars, we find our place.
With lullabies that gently weave,
A tapestry of dreams to leave.

Each soft embrace, a whisper sweet,
In slumber's hold, we feel complete.
Beneath the gaze of restful sights,
We drift away to endless nights.

Starlight and Moonbeams

In the quiet of night's embrace,
Stars whisper secrets, soft and bright.
Moonbeams dance with a gentle grace,
Guiding dreams in silver light.

Hearts alight with the glow above,
Each twinkle tells a tale anew.
Wrapped in the warmth of celestial love,
The night sky paints a canvas true.

Chasing shadows, we find our way,
Through the realm where wonders teem.
Starlight leads us, a soft ballet,
A journey born from every dream.

So let us wander, hand in hand,
Underneath the vast expanse.
In this luminous wonderland,
Together, we will forever dance.

A Tapestry Woven in Sleep

Threads of dreams spun soft and fine,
In the loom of night they intertwine.
Colors blend in visions deep,
Creating a tapestry while we sleep.

The fabric of time unfolds its wings,
Embracing the stories our day brings.
Each stitch a memory, a love so sweet,
Crafted in shadows where heartbeats meet.

As gentle sighs drift through the air,
Night weaves its magic, beyond compare.
In this slumber, peace we reap,
A world of wonder, woven in sleep.

Awake with morning's tender light,
The tapestry dances, vibrant and bright.
Reminding us of all we've dreamt,
A masterpiece, our hearts exempt.

The Quest for the Dream Weaver

On a journey through the twilight's haze,
We seek the Weaver of our dreams.
With every step, the world ablaze,
Caught within night's shimmering beams.

Whispers of magic lead the way,
Through enchanted forests, deep and wide.
The secrets of night, in soft array,
Guide us where woven hopes abide.

In the embrace of starlit skies,
We search for threads of hope and light.
With each heartbeat, our spirit flies,
Chasing shadows, igniting the night.

The Dream Weaver smiles, serene and wise,
As we unravel each tangled seam.
In this realm of infinite ties,
We find our strength, our truest dream.

A Meadow of Restful Wanderings

In a meadow where wildflowers sway,
Gentle breezes hum a tune.
The sun dips low at the end of day,
As dusk brings forth a silver moon.

Softly we tread on petals bright,
Lost in thoughts that wander free.
Each step a dance, pure delight,
In this haven, just you and me.

Crickets chirp their lullaby call,
While twilight wraps the world in peace.
Every worry begins to fall,
As nature grants our souls release.

Here we linger, hearts unfurled,\nIn the embrace of fading light.
A meadow where dreams are swirled,
In restful wanderings of the night.

Lullabies of the Starry Sky

In the night, the stars do gleam,
Whispers soft as a gentle stream.
The moonlight weaves a silver thread,
Cradling dreams in a cozy bed.

Clouds drift by like thoughts so light,
As nature sings her sweet goodnight.
Each twinkle holds a tale to tell,
In slumber's arms, we rest so well.

Adventures in Serenity's Embrace

In fields of green, we roam so free,
Where whispers of the wind agree.
Mountains call and rivers flow,
In serenity, our spirits grow.

Beneath the arch of endless sky,
We chase the dreams that soar up high.
Moments linger, pure and bright,
In the embrace of soothing night.

Dreamcatcher's Serenade

Softly now, the night unfolds,
A dreamcatcher catches hopes untold.
With every breath, we find our peace,
In this haven, worries cease.

The stars above begin to dance,
Inviting hearts to take a chance.
Every whisper, every sigh,
Echoes sweetly in the sky.

The Enchanted Slumber Journey

Close your eyes, let troubles fade,
In dreams, a magical parade.
Through valleys where the wildflowers sway,
We wander in a twilight play.

With gentle hands, the night takes hold,
Wraps us warm in stories bold.
Adventures await where shadows lie,
In the land of the lullaby.

Tales from the Midnight Clock

The hands do tick, a midnight tale,
Whispers run deep, where shadows sail.
Secrets held in the chime's soft ring,
Echoes of thoughts that night can bring.

Each tick a memory, faint and clear,
Stories woven from dreams held dear.
In the silent hours, magic takes flight,
Unraveling truths hidden from light.

Driftwood Dreams and Marshmallow Clouds

Driftwood lies on the golden shore,
Where dreams like waves come to explore.
Marshmallow clouds in the cerulean sky,
Whisper sweet nothings as they drift by.

Childhood laughter dances on the breeze,
While the world spins slow through swaying trees.
In this place, where wishes grow wide,
Heartfelt echoes in the ocean's tide.

Serenity's Secret Passage

In the stillness where silence flows,
A hidden path only the heart knows.
Softly it beckons to those who seek,
A tranquil whisper, serene and meek.

Through arching trees and the softest light,
Nature's embrace wraps the soul tight.
A journey inward, where peace resides,
In serenity's arms, the spirit glides.

The Wandering Souls of Slumber

Each night they wander, the souls at rest,
Drifting through dreams, on a quest blessed.
In twilight's hush, they rise and roam,
Seeking the magic that feels like home.

With starlit eyes and gentle grace,
They dance on moonbeams, a sacred space.
In the realm of dreams, where wishes flow,
The wandering souls find their way to glow.

Shadows Beneath the Bedroom Canopy

Silhouettes dance upon the walls,
Whispers of secrets, hidden calls.
Moonlight flickers, soft and bright,
Bathed in dreams, embracing night.

Curtains sway with a gentle breeze,
Cradling thoughts like fragile leaves.
In twilight's hush, the world slows down,
Wrapped in sleep, where peace is found.

Tucked Away in Dreamland

Close your eyes, drift to the skies,
In the land where magic lies.
Clouds of cotton, pillows of fluff,
In this realm, you have enough.

Stars sprinkle softly, guiding your way,
Through the night until break of day.
Tucked in tight, your worries cease,
In dreamland's arms, you find your peace.

Riding the Winds of Serenade

Melodies float on the evening air,
Carried by whispers—secrets rare.
On the wings of night, we glide,
In serenades, our hearts confide.

The world a stage, lit just for you,
Dancing shadows, a sight so true.
As stars hum sweet lullabies,
In this symphony, our spirits rise.

Tracing the Fables of Slumber Paths

Every dream a tale to weave,
Stories linger as we believe.
Through the night, paths intertwine,
In slumber's grasp, all is divine.

Footsteps echo on midnight trails,
Mapping journeys where love prevails.
Each fable whispers, softly known,
In the depths of night, dreams are sown.

Mystical Nights in Restful Haze

Beneath the silver moonlit sky,
Whispers of the stars all sigh.
In shadows deep, where spirits play,
A magic realm dreams night away.

The breeze carries secrets of the night,
Wrapped in a cloak of soft twilight.
Dancing leaves in a gentle sway,
Calling forth dreams that softly stay.

Fog rolls in, a tender embrace,
Cocooning hearts in a tranquil space.
Every breath, a lullaby's tune,
As we drift to where dreams are strewn.

Awake in the hush of the dawn's first light,
Where echoes of magic take flight.
The mystic night bids us goodbye,
But its sweet essence will always lie.

The Gentle Pursuit of Dreamy Delights

In the still of the night, we roam,
Chasing shadows of our own home.
Whispers of dreams begin to unfold,
Tales of wonder waiting to be told.

With each breath, we venture near,
To places where hearts have no fear.
Stars twinkle like lanterns in the deep,
Guiding us softly into sleep.

Waves of color brush the dark sky,
Painting visions that flutter and fly.
Every moment, a gentle caress,
Cradling souls in a warm, soft dress.

The night is a canvas, vast and wide,
Filled with the dreams we try to hide.
With each tender wave of the night's embrace,
We find our peace in this sacred space.

Floating Through the Fog of Slumber

Drifting softly on clouds of gray,
Wrapped in dreams that ebb and sway.
The fog whispers secrets just for us,
In the silence, we find our trust.

Each heartbeat echoes through the night,
Guiding us toward the fading light.
Floating high on the softest breeze,
Lost in the laughter of swaying trees.

As we wander through the misty veil,
Stories of wonder begin to sail.
Every flicker tells a tale anew,
Painting the night in shades of blue.

Awakening gently with dawn's caress,
Leaving behind the night's sweet stress.
In the echoes of dreams yet to come,
We find our peace as the day succumbs.

Tales from the Abyss of Nighttime

Whispers float in shadowed nights,
Secrets hidden from the sights.
The moon casts dreams upon the ground,
In quiet realms where hope is found.

Echoes call from distant deep,
Where ancient stories drift to sleep.
The stars alight with tales to share,
Of journeys bold and silent prayer.

Night unveils a mystic lore,
As dreams unlock the midnight door.
Beneath the sky, we dive and sway,
In enchanted realms, forever play.

Through darkness wide, our spirits soar,
To find the light on secret shore.
The abyss sings its lullaby sweet,
In twilight's arms, our hearts entreat.

Starlight Adventures of the Sleepy Heart

In starlit skies, the dreams take flight,
The sleepy hearts embrace the night.
With every twinkle, hope ignites,
Guiding souls through starry fights.

Along the paths where wishes flow,
Adventures bloom in soft moon glow.
Through silver beams, we dance and glide,
On cosmic tides, our fears subside.

The heart, though weary, swells with grace,
In every starlight's warm embrace.
With laughter shared, and courage bright,
We chart our course in gentle light.

In dreams we sail on distant seas,
Where every heart finds joy and peace.
The sleepy heart, forever free,
Adventures weave in harmony.

Pillow Forts and Starry Escapes

In pillow forts, a world unfolds,
With secrets wove in dreams of old.
Beneath the sheets, we find our way,
To distant lands where shadows play.

In starlit skies, the brave embark,
To seek the tales that leave a mark.
With every whisper, hearts align,
In cozy spaces, we intertwine.

Adventures spark in laughter's glow,
As night-time breezes gently blow.
Through fabric walls, imagination flies,
In cozy nooks where magic lies.

Together we weave a starry quest,
In pillow forts, we find our rest.
With dreams as wide as the endless night,
Our hearts create a world of light.

The Enchanted Snooze

When twilight falls and silence sings,
The enchanted snooze brings wondrous things.
Softly nestled in twilight's arms,
The world outside fades, pure still charms.

Adventures whispered in lullabies,
Dance in the depths of sleepy sighs.
With every breath, the magic grows,
In slumber's grasp, our essence flows.

Through dreamlit realms, we drift and roam,
In the enchanted snooze, we find our home.
Where wishes bloom and fears take flight,
In this embrace, we own the night.

So close your eyes and take the leap,
Into the bliss of dreams so deep.
The enchanted snooze awaits your heart,
In slumber's realm, we'll never part.

An Odyssey in the Realm of Dozing

In slumber's realm, we drift away,
Beneath the stars, where shadows play.
Each whispered dream, a gentle guide,
In soft embrace, our fears subside.

Waves of rest, a tender sea,
Where time forgets, and hearts are free.
A journey far, yet close at hand,
In dozing's path, we understand.

The night unfolds its velvet shroud,
In quietude, we weave the loud.
Each sigh and breath, a sacred song,
In this deep hush, we all belong.

So close your eyes, let worries cease,
Embark with me, and find your peace.
An odyssey of dreams unchained,
In dozing's arms, we'll be sustained.

Cradled by Night's Whispering Wings

The moonlight spills on gentle streams,
As night unfolds its quiet dreams.
Cradled softly in twilight's arms,
We find the calm, the soothing charms.

The world fades out, a distant hum,
In slumber's grace, our minds succumb.
With every breath, the shadows creep,
Awakening desires in our sleep.

The stars, they wink with knowing eyes,
As whispered secrets fill the skies.
Each feathered thought begins to soar,
In night's embrace, we ask for more.

Cradled tight by dreams untold,
In silver light, our futures unfold.
With every sigh, the night draws near,
A symphony of peace to hear.

Unveiling the Curtain of Dreams

Behind the curtain, shadows stir,
A world of wonders starts to purr.
Each thought a flicker, bright and bold,
Unraveling tales, both new and old.

With gentle hands, the night unfolds,
A tapestry of dreams and gold.
Visions beckon from realms of night,
In whispered tones, they take their flight.

We dance through realms of soft delight,
Awakening glimmers in the night.
The curtain parts, revealing all,
In dreams we rise, in dreams we fall.

So close your eyes, let visions stream,
Together we will weave and dream.
Unveiling tales that spin and play,
In night's embrace, we drift away.

Moonbeams and the Quest for Comfort

Moonbeams dance on silver lakes,
In soothing light, the stillness wakes.
The night enfolds with tender care,
A quest for comfort, ever rare.

Through gentle waves, our spirits glide,
On whispered winds, we'll gently ride.
Each silken thread of twilight's breath,
Wraps us in love, denying death.

A starry map, our dreams in flight,
Exploring shadows, chasing light.
In every corner, solace found,
A quiet peace, both deep and profound.

Moonbeams guide us from afar,
In night's embrace, we know just who we are.
With each heartbeat, we draw near,
A quest for comfort, always here.

Moonlit Paths and Drowsy Trails

Under the moon's gentle gaze,
Shadows dance in soft embrace.
Whispers of night fill the air,
Guiding footsteps without a care.

Winding trails bathed in silver,
Each step a secret to unravel.
The heart beats slow and steady,
In this world prepared and ready.

Stars twinkle above in cheer,
Nature's melody, pure and clear.
With dreams that drift like mist,
On these paths, all worries cease.

In drowsy trails, time stands still,
With every turn, a chance to feel.
Lost in wonder, lost in grace,
On moonlit paths, we find our place.

Exploring the Land of Quiet Murmurs

In the land where whispers roam,
Softly calling you back home.
Gentle winds weave through the trees,
Rustling leaves in secret pleas.

Here, no rush, just tranquil bliss,
Every sigh a silent kiss.
To explore this quiet song,
Is to know where we belong.

Footsteps light on earthy ground,
Magic hidden all around.
With each shadow, tales unfold,
In quiet murmurs, stories told.

The heart finds peace in every glance,
In this sleepy, slow romance.
As the dawn begins to rise,
Hope awakens in the skies.

A Voyage through the Velvet Night

As velvet skies stretch far and wide,
Dreamers sail on starlit tides.
With courage wrapped in twilight's hue,
A voyage calls, invitation true.

Waves of whispers softly blend,
Cascading moments, no need to mend.
The moon, our lantern, guides the way,
Through mysteries that softly sway.

In this vast, enchanting sea,
Every star a memory.
Lost horizons beckon near,
In the night, all roads are clear.

Together we drift, hearts set free,
On this voyage, just you and me.
As night unfolds its tender charms,
We wander safe in each other's arms.

Soft Echoes of a Dreamscape

In a dreamscape, soft and bright,
Echoes linger in the night.
Colors blend in twilight's grace,
Creating worlds we long to chase.

Whispers weave through melting skies,
Where fantasy in silence lies.
Every sigh, a soft embrace,
In this realm of endless space.

The heartbeats pulse in rhythmic song,
In the places where we belong.
Floating softly, lost in light,
On these echoes, we take flight.

Through every doorway, dreams unfold,
Stories brighter than purest gold.
In soft echoes, we find our way,
Guided by the light of day.

A Voyage to the Dreaming Isle

Upon the sea of whispers, we sail,
With stars our guides, on a moonlit trail.
The waves sing tales of the night's embrace,
While dreams unfold in this sacred space.

The wind carries laughter, soft and light,
As we drift through the canvas of night.
Isle of slumber, where wishes take flight,
In the arms of dreams, everything feels right.

The horizon glows with a gentle hue,
Painting the sky with the day's adieu.
In the distance, a lullaby calls,
Leading us into the night's soft thralls.

Here, time is lost, a fleeting mirage,
In the dreaming isle, we find our collage.
With each heartbeat, a promise is spun,
A voyage to dreams has only begun.

Shadows Dance in Moonlight's Glow

In the quiet night, shadows weave,
Under the moon, they dance and leave.
A delicate rhythm, so wild, untamed,\nIn the soft luminance, they are unclaimed.

Whispers of secrets float through the air,
Each twirl and twist, a silent dare.
The night wraps around like a velvet cloak,
As the darkness breathes with each gentle stroke.

Branches sway, casting stories anew,
While twinkling stars join the shadows' brew.
A union of dreams under silver skies,
Where silence reigns and the heart complies.

In this realm where the wild things play,
The moon's soft glow lights the way.
Together we dance, with spirits so free,
In the shadows' embrace, just you and me.

The Sleepy Traveler's Maze

In a town that sleeps, paths start to fade,
Where the stars flicker softly, a whispering trade.
Each corner beckons with stories untold,
In the sleepy traveler's maze to behold.

Cobblestones glisten with the dew of night,
As lanterns flicker, casting shadows bright.
Lost in the alleys of dreams yet to chase,
Time slips away in this quiet embrace.

Wandering souls in the hush of the hour,
Finding solace in night's tender power.
Lost in our thoughts, where silence is loud,
As we dance through the mist, unshackled, unbowed.

Through twisting paths and turns, we glide,
With the moon above, our silent guide.
In the maze of the night, we will find our way,
To the dawn that awaits, at the break of day.

Secrets of the Drowsy Grove

In the grove where the willows weep,
Lies a realm where secrets sleep.
Midnight blooms in the softest glow,
Whispering tales of the winds that flow.

A drowsy hush wraps each gentle bough,
As time stands still in the night's soft vow.
Hidden echoes of laughter and sighs,
In the heart of the grove, where magic lies.

Crickets hum in a melodious tone,
Guiding lost souls to a world unknown.
Each step a story, each gaze a dream,
In the drowsy grove, nothing's as it seems.

Under the stars, the secrets unfold,
In shadows and whispers, adventures are told.
Together we wander, in moonlight we roam,
In the secrets of the grove, we find our home.

Let Us Dance with the Dreaming Moon

In the glow of night so bright,
We twirl beneath the silver light.
Stars whisper secrets to the sky,
As we dance where shadows lie.

With each step, the world fades away,
Lost in time, where dreams hold sway.
The moon smiles down from up above,
Guiding us with warmth and love.

Whirling petals in the breeze,
Nature's songs, our hearts appease.
With every twinkle in the night,
We dream, we laugh, we feel delight.

So let us dance, oh come what may,
Together in this grand ballet.
With the dreaming moon as our guide,
In this moment, let hope reside.

In Search of the Midnight Castle

Upon the hill where shadows creep,
A castle sleeps, its secrets keep.
Through tangled woods and misty trails,
We seek the stories, hear the tales.

Each stone a whisper of the past,
Echoes of laughter, shadows cast.
With every step, the night draws near,
Adventure beckons, crystal clear.

The moonlight dances on the walls,
As silence reigns in ancient halls.
What wonders lie just out of sight,
In this enchanted, starry night?

So come with me, let dreams take flight,
To find the castle in the night.
With hearts ablaze and spirits free,
We'll carve our names in history.

Sails of Slumber on Soft Waters

Gentle waves beneath the stars,
Whispers drift from near and far.
Sails of slumber catch the breeze,
Cradling dreams amidst the trees.

Moonlit paths like silver threads,
Guiding us where calmness spreads.
With every glide, the night unfurls,
A tapestry of starlit pearls.

In the quiet, hearts align,
Floating softly, feeling fine.
Ripples echo lullabies,
As we sail beneath the skies.

So let us drift on water deep,
Embracing peace, layer of sleep.
With sails of dreams that softly soar,
We find our haven evermore.

Whimsical Dreams and Wandering Hearts

In a world where wonders bloom,
We dance and laugh, dispelling gloom.
Whimsical dreams forever twirl,
Calling forth the magic swirl.

With wandering hearts, we chart our course,
Exploring life with boundless force.
Each moment glimmers, bright and bold,
As we embark on journeys told.

Laughter echoes, colors play,
In the chase of night and day.
With open arms and joyful cheer,
We cherish every moment here.

So let us weave our stories fine,
In the fabric of the divine.
With whimsical dreams and hearts so free,
Together, we'll create our symphony.

Whispers of the Dreaming Woods

In the woods where shadows play,
Gentle whispers lead the way.
Leaves that rustle, secrets share,
Softly calling, magic rare.

Moonlight dances on the ground,
In this realm, dreams can be found.
Each step taken, whispers sigh,
Underneath the starlit sky.

Creatures murmur ancient tales,
Echoing through misty vales.
Nature's voice, a sacred hymn,
Guiding souls who wander in.

Embrace the night, let go of fear,
In this place, all is clear.
Whispers call, sweet and low,
In the woods where dreams do grow.

Journey into the Land of Slumber

Close your eyes, the journey starts,
To the land where stillness imparts.
Clouds of cotton, soft and white,
Floating gently through the night.

Drift through valleys rich and deep,
Where shadows sigh and starlights weep.
Each breath taken brings you near,
To the dreams waiting here.

Through the fields of silken gold,
Stories of the night unfold.
Every thought, a guiding star,
Leading you wherever you are.

Awake anew when morning gleams,
From the depths of silent dreams.
With each dawn, a gift so clear,
The journey beckons, drawing near.

Stars Beneath Closed Eyes

In the silence where dreams reside,
Stars are blooming deep inside.
Close your eyes, let darkness reign,
Imagination breaks the chain.

Patterns form in the quiet space,
Galaxies dance in a gentle embrace.
Whispers echo, soft and bright,
Painting visions in the night.

Each pulse of thought, a shooting star,
Carving paths to lands afar.
With every heartbeat, worlds collide,
In the universe where dreams abide.

So drift away on waves of light,
Chasing stars till morning's height.
In this realm, let spirit soar,
Find the magic evermore.

The Quest for the Midnight Blanket

Underneath the moon's soft glow,
Adventurers brave set to go.
Through the valleys, over hills,
Seeking warmth the midnight fills.

Whispers guide with gentle hand,
Leading to the hidden land.
Where the stars weave tapestries,
Of dreams entwined in silver seas.

Every step a quest unfolds,
For the blanket that gently holds.
Magic threads of night and light,
Wrapped in dreams, soft and bright.

Finding solace in the weave,
Together in what we believe.
With the dawn, our hearts are free,
Questing still, for unity.

Twilight Journeys in a Land of Dreams

In the hush of day's soft end,
Whispers of twilight gently wend.
Stars peek out, a shy delight,
Guiding hearts into the night.

Crickets sing a lullaby,
While silver clouds drift softly by.
Each moment holds a sacred grace,
In the dreamscape's warm embrace.

Footsteps follow the moonlit trail,
Where shadowed secrets softly sail.
Every sigh a wish we weave,
In the twilight, we believe.

Horizon calls, a journey vast,
Echoes of futures, present, past.
Through the silence, echoing dreams,
Twilight whispers, all is as it seems.

The Wondering Eyes of Midnight

Midnight's cloak wraps around tight,
With wandering eyes that seek the light.
Stars twinkle like secrets held,
In silence, every heart is compelled.

Within the still, a question burns,
What lessons do the shadows learn?
Each heartbeat, a drum, a quest,
As dreams awaken from their rest.

The moon, a guardian in the skies,
Watches over these wondering eyes.
Every glance, a story spun,
In the night, we are all one.

As whispers blend with the cool night air,
Each thought a feather, soft as prayer.
Midnight's charm, a spell we chase,
In the stillness, we find our place.

Slumber's Serenade: A Quest for Rest

In the arms of night we lie,
While the stars begin to sigh.
Dreams emerge like tender songs,
Guiding us where hope belongs.

Pillows cradling weary heads,
Whispers dance where silence spreads.
In twilight's arms, our worries cease,
As slumber grants the soul its peace.

Each breath a note in night's sweet song,
We drift to where the lost belong.
In twilight's fold, we seek the rest,
Within the stillness, we are blessed.

With every yawn, the dreams take flight,
On gentle wings through the quiet night.
A quest for rest, a serenade,
Where heartbeats linger, unafraid.

Where the Shadows Dance with Sleep

In the quiet where shadows creep,
Life unveils the joy of sleep.
Beneath the stars, they swirl and sway,
In a soft and silken ballet.

Within the haze of slumber's reach,
Wisdom whispered, lessons teach.
Every sigh a breeze set free,
In this realm, we find the key.

The moonlight glimmers, a silver thread,
Stitching dreams in twilight's bed.
Where shadows dance, our spirits rise,
In this sacred realm, we realize.

As night unfolds her velvet wing,
In dreams, our hearts begin to sing.
Where the shadows dance, take heed,
In their embrace, we plant the seed.

Moonlit Trails of Dreams

Beneath a silent silver glow,
The stars whisper tales untold,
In shadows where the soft winds blow,
A wanderer's heart grows bold.

Through silvered branches, whispers weave,
A dance of light upon the ground,
In every sigh, the dreamers believe,
While nature's song is gently found.

Along the path where shadows gleam,
Footprints trace the night so bright,
With every step, we weave a dream,
And fold the dark into the light.

Awakened by the morning's call,
The dreams retreat with dawn's embrace,
Yet in our hearts, they leave a thrall,
The moonlit trails, a sacred place.

The Slumbering Sea and Hidden Shores

The sea sings softly to the moon,
In whispers of a timeless song,
The waves embrace their sweet cocoon,
As night drapes all where dreams belong.

Beneath the calm, the secrets lie,
Of treasures lost and hopes reclaimed,
Where every tide can say goodbye,
While hidden shores await unclaimed.

Stars glance down at waters deep,
A dance of light on rippling tides,
In quiet depths, where shadows creep,
The soul of the slumbering sea hides.

Awake, the dawn unveils the past,
A shining world of azure bright,
In every wave, a moment cast,
The hidden shores in morning light.

Navigating the Clouds of Imagination

In skies where dreams and visions meet,
Clouds drift and swirl in endless play,
With every thought, we rise, we fleet,
On wings of hope, we fly away.

The sun paints dreams in pastel hues,
Each thought takes flight, a brand new start,
In gentle winds, we chase the blues,
Creating worlds from purest art.

With starlit paths and guiding lights,
We sail through realms yet to explore,
In fleeting moments, pure delights,
Our hearts embrace what's meant for more.

And when the shadows call us down,
We'll cherish clouds of yesteryears,
For in our minds, we wear no crown,
Just whispers soft, and flowing tears.

The Echoes of Silent Slumbers

In twilight's grasp, the silence falls,
Dreams whisper low, inviting peace,
As echoes roam through shadowed halls,
Where every heartbeat finds release.

The night unfolds its tender shroud,
With velvet stars that softly gleam,
In every sigh, a secret loud,
Awakens in the shades of dream.

When dawn awakens, echoes fade,
Yet in our hearts, their warmth survives,
In quietude, the fears are laid,
In silent slumbers, still we thrive.

For every whisper, soft and deep,
In shadows graced by time's embrace,
We wander through the paths of sleep,
And find ourselves in dreams' trace.

The Dreamcatcher's Mysterious Map

In whispers soft, the night unfolds,
A map of dreams in silver holds.
Paths of shadows, trails of light,
Guiding hearts through starry night.

Wanderers seek what lies ahead,
In tangled threads, their hopes are fed.
Each stitch a wish, each knot a tale,
In slumber's grasp, they softly sail.

Beyond the veil where visions twine,
The dreamcatcher weaves a sacred sign.
With every loop, the stories grow,
An endless journey, shadows flow.

Underneath the moon's embrace,
The mystery drawn, a secret place.
Upon this map, their spirits soar,
To realms unknown, forevermore.

Drowsy Wonders Beneath the Milky Way

Beneath the sky where whispers hum,
Drowsy wonders softly come.
Heaven's dust, a gentle sway,
Dreamers drift in soft ballet.

Galaxies spin, a cosmic dance,
In night's embrace, they find their chance.
Starlit tales in twilight's glow,
Awaken hearts where shadows flow.

Clouds of dreams like feathers fall,
Each a secret, a silent call.
Shimmering lights in the velvet sea,
Guide the lost to what will be.

Sweet lullabies from ages past,
In this stillness, dreams hold fast.
Drowsy wonders cradle the night,
Framed in the Milky Way's soft light.

Celestial Sojourns in Starlit Calm

Celestial sojourns in the night,
Stars map the way, a twinkling light.
Quiet whispers in the breeze,
Time drifts by with graceful ease.

In stillness deep, the cosmos breathes,
Nurtured by mysteries the universe weaves.
Comets trail through endless heights,
Guiding those with lost delights.

Every glance, a world awakes,
Colorful dreams a heart remakes.
Wrapped in calm, under the sky,
Seeking truths where the echoes lie.

Soft reflections on the lake,
Pathways branching, souls awake.
Celestial journeys, vast and grand,
Hand in hand, we'll understand.

The Adventure of Drowsy Souls

In twilight's mist, the drowsy roam,
Seeking shelter, finding home.
Souls adrift in dreams untold,
Chasing shadows, brave and bold.

Each step whispers of the past,
Echoes fading, shadows cast.
A journey carved in starlit haze,
Winding paths through the moon's gaze.

Lullabies from time's embrace,
Guide them onward, set the pace.
With every heartbeat, hope ignites,
In the adventure of starry nights.

Fleeting moments kissed by grace,
The drowsy souls find their place.
Chasing dreams beneath the stars,
Their spirits dance, forever ours.

Cloud Castles and Whispered Tales

In the sky, dreams take flight,
Cloud castles shimmer bright.
Whispers dance on gentle breeze,
Telling tales among the trees.

Stars twinkle in twilight's embrace,
Soft shadows drift, find their place.
Golden rays of the setting sun,
Guide the heart, the tale's begun.

Laughter echoes, children play,
In the clouds, they drift and sway.
Imaginations run so free,
In this land of mystery.

As night falls, dreams unfold,
Whispered tales of love untold.
In the quiet, magic weaves,
A world where every soul believes.

The Odyssey of Drowsy Delights.

Close your eyes, the voyage starts,
Sailing on with sleepy hearts.
Waves of calm, a soothing song,
In this dreamland, we belong.

Clouds like pillows, soft and light,
Guiding us through starry night.
Each moment, a delight to taste,
In this realm where dreams won't waste.

Whispers low of secrets old,
Drowsy delights in stories told.
Magic mushrooms, moonlit streams,
In the shadows, weave our dreams.

The horizon fades, colors blend,
A journey where no time can end.
With sleepy eyes, we sail away,
In drowsy bliss, we drift and sway.

Whispers of a Dreamy Odyssey

Beneath the stars, the night awakes,
Whispers of dreams, the silence breaks.
Gentle winds, soft as a sigh,
Carry the tales that float on high.

In twilight's glow, shadows play,
Painting stories, night turns to day.
Misty horizons, a canvas wide,
Where whispers of dreams quietly glide.

Flowing rivers, glimmering tides,
In this wonder, the heart confides.
Every star, a whispered spark,
Leading us through the silent dark.

With each breath, the journey grows,
In this odyssey, our spirit flows.
So close your eyes, embrace the sea,
For the whispers beckon you and me.

Clouds of Slumber's Embrace

Beneath soft clouds, we find our peace,
In slumber's arms, our worries cease.
Dreams unfold like petals bright,
Guided by the silver light.

Hush now, world, let silence reign,
In this moment, free from pain.
Each breath a whisper, soft and slow,
In the embrace of night's warm glow.

Floating high on a sea of dreams,
With every thought, reality seems.
Clouds cradle us, tender and light,
As we wander through the night.

As dawn approaches, light cascades,
Colors burst, in splendor, parades.
But in our hearts, the dreams remain,
In clouds of slumber, free from strain.

Trails of Comfort in a Dreamy Grove

Whispers of leaves dance with grace,
Soft shadows play on my face.
Birds sing sweetly, hidden from view,
In this grove where dreams come true.

Gentle breezes carry my soul,
Nature's magic makes me whole.
Steps on trails, both light and free,
Finding comfort, just me and the trees.

Sunlight filters through the green,
Each moment feels serene.
In this haven, I'm not alone,
The grove cradles me like a home.

With every turn, new wonders ignite,
In this dreamy space, all feels right.
I wander deeper, heart aglow,
Each trail leads to the love I know.

Finding Peace on a Cloudy Trail

Gray skies blanket the winding path,
A calmness settles; I find my breath.
Footsteps padding on soft, damp earth,
Each step whispers of quiet worth.

Clouds embrace the hills around,
Nature's hush is all I've found.
In this maze of misty gray,
I seek the peace that leads my way.

A gentle lull, the world feels slow,
With every stride, my worries go.
Soft echoes of nature guide me through,
On this cloudy trail, I find what's true.

The beauty lies in stillness found,
Each raindrop's kiss a soothing sound.
Beneath the clouds, I learn to trust,
Finding peace is a must.

A Secret Journey through Drowsiness

In the haze of twilight's gleam,
I drift softly into a dream.
The world blurs as I wander deep,
In the land where shadows sleep.

Whispers call from hidden glades,
Soft songs play in dusky shades.
Each step is light; I float like air,
In this journey, free from care.

Through ethereal woods, I roam,
In the stillness, I feel at home.
Golden hues of fading light,
Guide my heart through velvet night.

In drowsiness, secrets are spun,
Lost in dreams, I become one.
Every sigh, every gentle breeze,
Embraces me, my thoughts at ease.

The Chronicles of Slumber's Embrace

In the quiet hours of night,
Slumber wraps me, soft and light.
Tales unfold in dreams I weave,
Adventurous journeys I believe.

Stars whisper secrets from above,
In this quiet, I'm filled with love.
Each chapter unfolds in hues so bright,
Guided by the moon's kind light.

Through lands of wonder, I take flight,
Chasing shadows, dancing in delight.
Every dream, a legacy spun,
In slumber's arms, I am never done.

With sunrise casts, the tales may fade,
Yet in my heart, the magic stayed.
The chronicles of dreams embrace,
A treasure found in slumber's grace.

Nightfall's Playground of Fantasies

When twilight whispers soft and low,
   Dancing shadows start to grow.
   Dreams awaken from their rest,
  In this realm, we are the guests.

  Moonlit paths we wander wide,
With our dreams as faithful guide.
    Every corner holds a tale,
   In this night, we shall not fail.

  Mystic creatures, bold and bright,
    Join our revels in the night.
Laughter echoes through the trees,
  As we sway with gentle breeze.

  Stars like lanterns, shining clear,
  Casting wonder, banishing fear.
  In this playground, we are free,
Chasing dreams by night's decree.

Tales from the Slumbering Woods

In the woods where silence droops,
Gentle spirits weave their loops.
Tales of wonder softly flow,
Where the moon's soft glow will show.

Beneath the boughs of ancient trees,
Whispers drift upon the breeze.
Echoes of a time long past,
In this slumber, shadows cast.

Creatures stir with sleepy eyes,
Underneath the starry skies.
Each star a story held so tight,
In the heart of dreamy night.

Rest your head on nature's breast,
In this realm, we find our rest.
As the woods hum lullabies,
Lost in tales, where magic lies.

Beneath the Starlit Canopy of Z's

Beneath the sky where starlight gleams,
Sleepy souls drift into dreams.
A canvas vast with dark and light,
Whispers lull the stars goodnight.

Night unveils its shimmering veil,
In this slumber, hearts won't fail.
Pillows soft and blankets warm,
Wrap us snug in night's embrace, calm.

Each twinkling star a wish in flight,
Guiding dreams through silent night.
Floating on clouds, we explore,
Endless realms forevermore.

As we drift in dreams divine,
Boundless worlds await to shine.
In this twilight, all is peace,
Beneath the stars, our joys increase.

A Nap in the Enchanted Kingdom

In a kingdom, lush and green,
Fairy tales are often seen.
Close your eyes, let the magic flow,
As the gentle breezes blow.

Crickets sing a soothing tune,
Rocking us beneath the moon.
Every corner holds a dream,
In the land of magic's gleam.

Resting on the soft, bright grass,
Time and worries gently pass.
Each petal holds a whispered cheer,
In this kingdom, free from fear.

Awakening in twilight's glow,
Through the meadows, spirits flow.
In this nap, our hearts take flight,
In the kingdom of pure light.

Slumbering Spirits and Magic Dreams

In the hush of night's embrace,
Spirits dance in moonlit grace.
Dreams weave soft as silken threads,
Carrying whispers from the dead.

Stars twinkle in a velvet sky,
While shadows murmur, softly sigh.
Magic flows in gentle streams,
Guiding souls through gentle dreams.

With every breath a story starts,
Resting deep within our hearts.
In slumber's hold, we find our way,
To realms of wonder, night and day.

As dawn arrives, the spirits fade,
Yet in our dreams, their paths are laid.
Awake, we carry echoes bright,
Of slumbering spirits in the night.

Wandering in a Sea of Serene Haze

Amidst the fog, where silence brews,
I wander softly, seeking clues.
A sea of dreams pulls me below,
In tranquil depths, I ebb and flow.

Gentle whispers call my name,
Each step I take, a fleeting game.
The air is thick with mystic lore,
As I drift on this cloudy shore.

Floating visions grace my sight,
Glowing softly in the night.
Every heartbeat feels so free,
Lost within this reverie.

The haze embraces, wraps me tight,
Guiding lost souls through the night.
In this sea, I lose my fears,
And find my heart among the years.

The Sleepy Expedition of Forgotten Tales

Beneath the stars, the stories lie,
In every glance, a map to try.
Explorers of a dreaming land,
With sleepy eyes, we take our stand.

Forgotten tales in whispers flow,
With every turn, more depths to know.
Adventurers in realms of night,
Chasing echoes, seeking light.

The sagas sung by unseen bards,
Were once engraved on ancient yards.
Legends walk with shadows by,
In sleepy realms where past souls sigh.

So close your eyes, take up the quest,
In dreams we find the very best.
Through winding paths and stories old,
We sail on waves of tales retold.

When Whispers of Night Roam Free

When the moon casts its silver glow,
And stars like secrets softly show.
Whispers of night begin to rise,
Filling the air with lullabies.

In the silence, shadows creep,
Delicate vows, the stars will keep.
Every flicker holds a desire,
As dreams ignite a gentle fire.

The clock ticks softly in the night,
Guiding hearts towards the light.
With every rustle, stories unfold,
In the arms of night, so brave and bold.

Let the whispers take you away,
Beyond the dawn, where spirits play.
In this realm where night runs deep,
We find our way—lost souls in sleep.

Milton Keynes UK
Ingram Content Group UK Ltd.
UKHW021129021124
450571UK00005B/84

9 789916 903605